The Little Egg
That Did Not Hatch

Written by
Beryl Mitchell, Ed.D.

with Illustrations by
Roederick Vines

Archway Publishing books may be ordered through booksellers or by contacting:

Archway Publishing
1663 Liberty Drive
Bloomington, IN 47403
www.archwaypublishing.com
1 (888) 242-5904

Because of the dynamic nature of the Internet, any web addresses or links contained in this book may have changed since publication and may no longer be valid. The views expressed in this work are solely those of the author and do not necessarily reflect the views of the publisher, and the publisher hereby disclaims any responsibility for them.

Illustrations by Roederick Vines

ISBN: 978-1-4808-2750-9 (sc)
ISBN: 978-1-4808-2751-6 (hc)
ISBN: 978-1-4808-2752-3 (e)

Print information available on the last page.

Archway Publishing rev. date: 5/6/2016

It is early spring and mommy is
busy cleaning and gardening.

And she finds a nest that she thought was
a ball of straw that had blown into her
yard during the cold winter winds.

Mommy looked and listened to
the sound of early spring.

Birds chirping, flowers
and trees opening their perfectly formed buds.

She realized what she thought was a ball
of straw was indeed a nest on her grill.

The nest resembled a horn of plenty that sometimes is used during Thanksgiving.

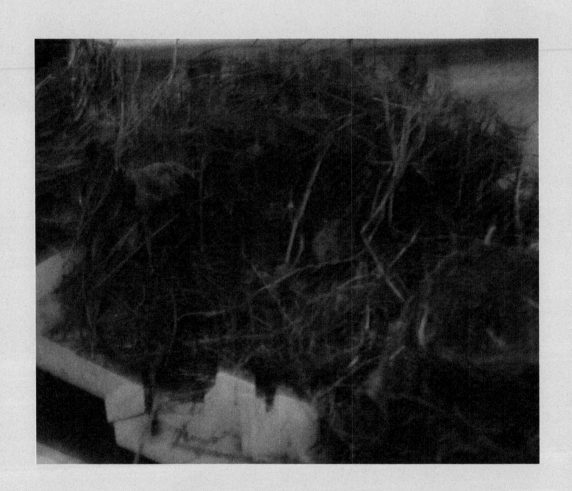

So excited she went to get her two little
boys to see the unusually shaped nest.

They watched the two baby birds grow strong.

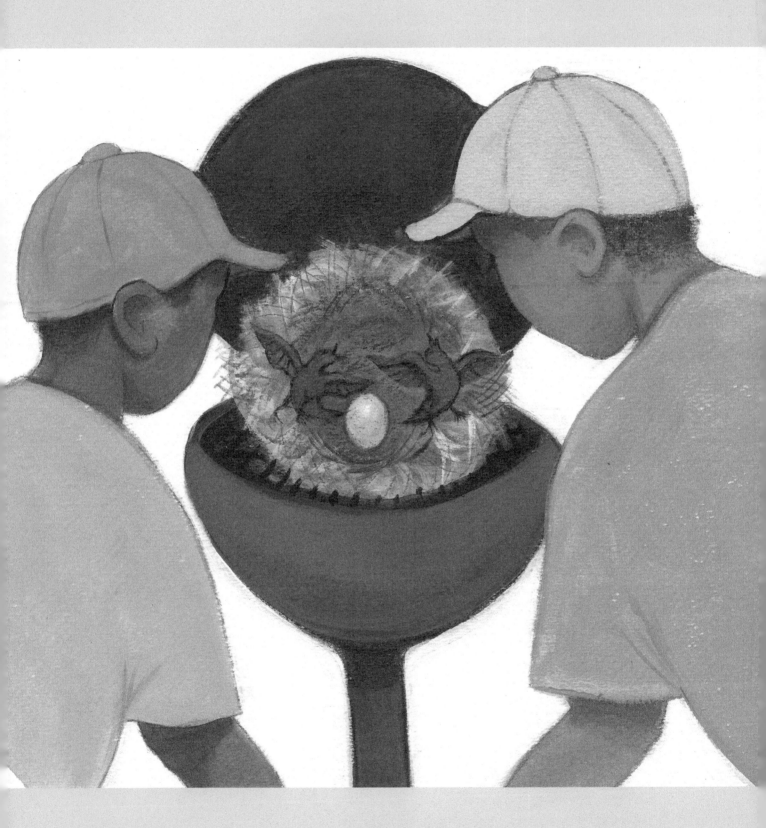

One day, two birds flew away.

The third baby bird was not healthy enough to grow.

The little boys wanted to save the
nest until the next spring.

So, they brought the nest into their home.

Mommy looked into the nest, and

discovered one tiny blue egg
resting at the end of the nest.

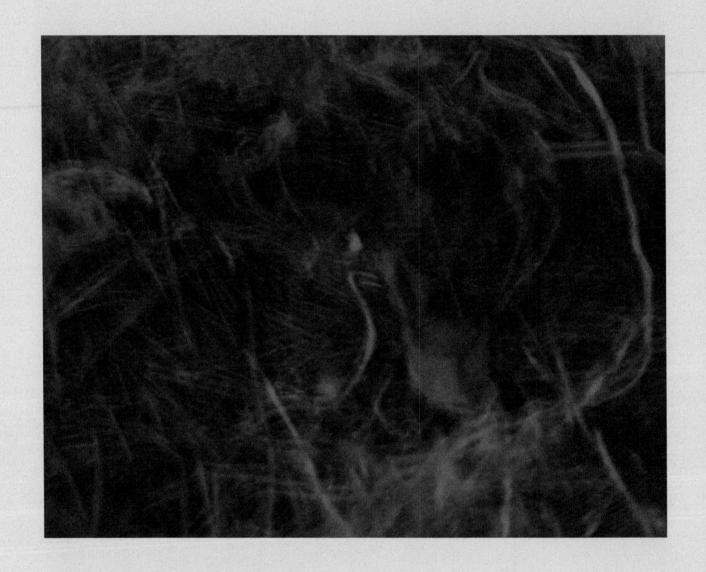

She explained to the children that sometimes eggs don't hatch if there is something wrong with the baby bird. Its nature's way, she further explained.

Her baby boy thought he could help the baby bird by removing it from the nest.

While trying to remove the egg with
his tiny fingers, he crushed the egg.

His mommy told him and his brother
not to worry about the egg.

The mommy Carolina Wren had done
everything possible to help her baby bird
to grow into a strong healthy bird.

Maybe next year she will return, build
a new nest, and lay another brood.
The cycle of life starts all over.

"Goodnight Brian and Dameon,"
said their mommy.

"Goodnight little birds where ever you are."

Parent information

- Always read your child's book first before sharing it.
- All new words such as brood (baby birds) should be discussed before you begin.
- Show them pictures of other nests. Some male birds take turns sitting on the nest while others help build the nest. Some birds lay more than one brood during the spring.
- Take them to the zoo to see different birds. Discuss the natural habitat of birds. Birds need food, water, and a safe place to fly to when a predator is present.
- Place a bird feeder in your yard.
- Purchase a guide to identify birds in your community.
- Remember, your children are little for a short period of time. Reading to your child daily creates a bond that neither you nor your child will ever forget.

About the Author

Beryl Mitchell is a native of Inkster, Michigan where she was educated in the public schools. She is a graduate of the prestigious Spelman College where she holds a degree in Child Development. Additionally, she has a Master of Arts in Special Education.

Dr. Mitchell earned her Ed.D. in 1992. She has also worked at Spelman College. Presently, she is employed by the Dekalb County Schools as an educator.

Dr. Mitchell is also a volunteer with the YMCA of USA and Coalition where she provides educational programs to schools in South Africa.

She is married and has two young adult sons.

About the Artist

Roederick Vines has illustrated
for books, magazines, books of the
Spoken Word and children books.

He is an award winning exhibiting artist
whose paintings are collected by many
across the country and the world. Mr. Vines
attended the Columbus College of Art and
Design and currently exhibits his paintings
in museums, galleries and private showings.

CPSIA information can be obtained
at www.ICGtesting.com
Printed in the USA
LVOW05s1703230616

493744LV00047B/383/P